Wyoming

ABC Coloring Book

An ABC Learning Activity Book all about Wyoming

With Count-to-10 Coloring Bonus!

Little Red Hills

Written & designed by: Rianna M. Hill

www.WyomingisHome.com

Wyoming is Home is a Brand of

Little Red Hills LLC

©2023

My ABCs Wyoming Coloring Book

name:

A

Antelope

Pronghorn antelope are the fastest land animal in North America, running up to 60 miles per hour.

B

Bison

Bison are the largest mammals in North America, and calves weigh 30–70 pounds at birth.

C Cowboy

Wyoming's nickname is the "Cowboy State"

D

Devil's Tower

Towering 1,267 feet over the river,
Devil's Tower is the largest example
of columnar jointing in the world.

E

Elk

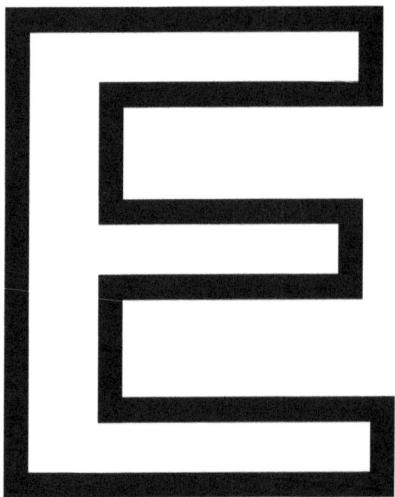

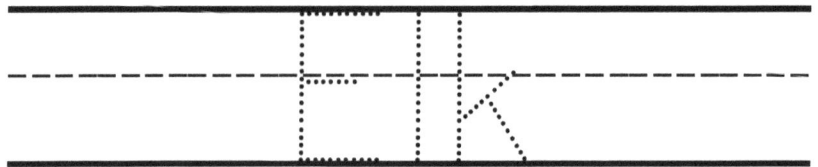

Males are known as bulls and weigh about 700 pounds and the females, called cows, weigh an average 500 pounds.

F

Fence

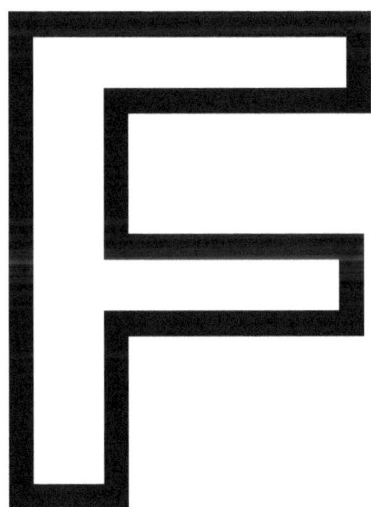

There are over 400 miles of snow
fences in Wyoming along the
roads.

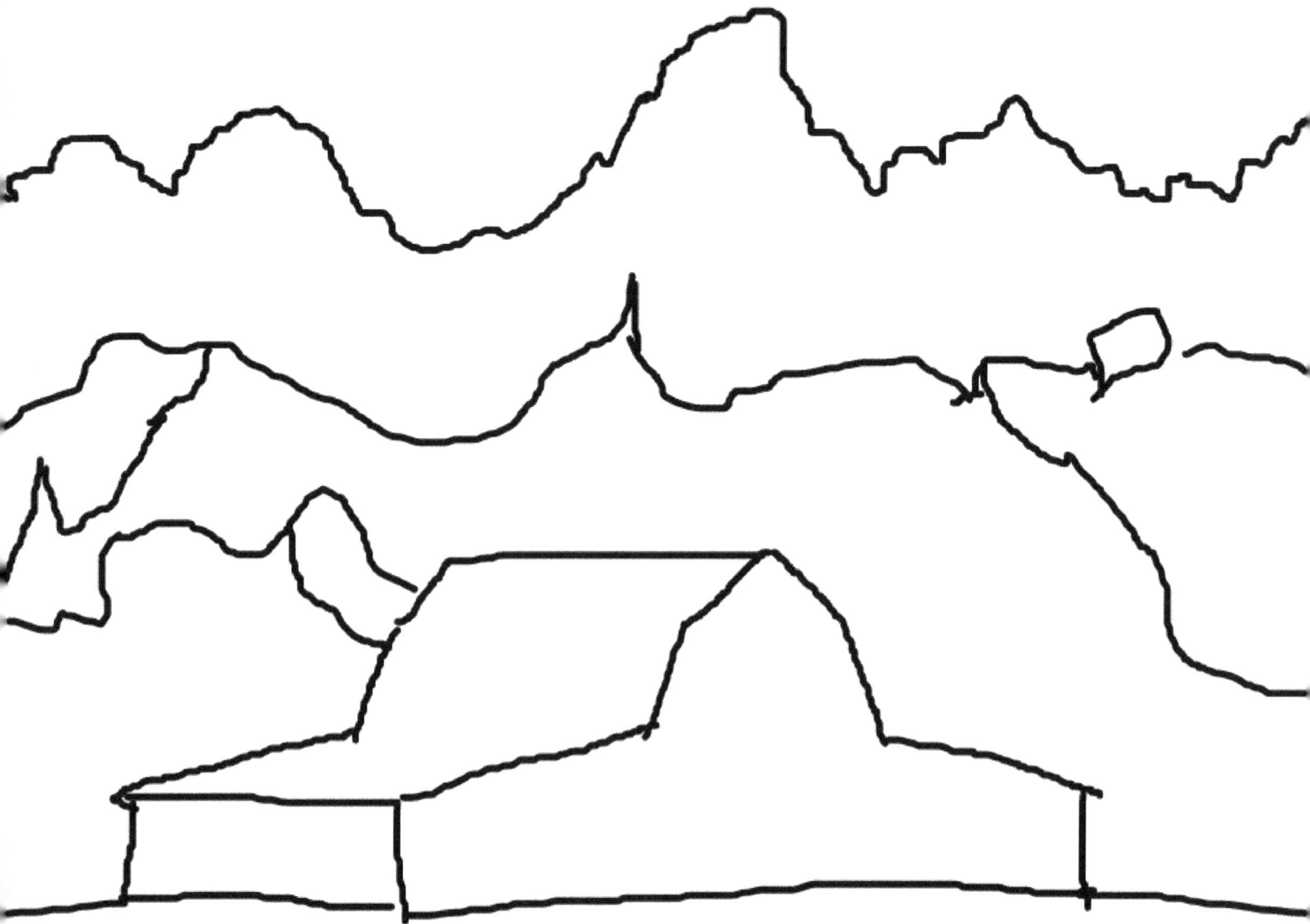

G

This National Park includes the 40-mile-long Teton Range which was created by earthquakes.

H

Horse

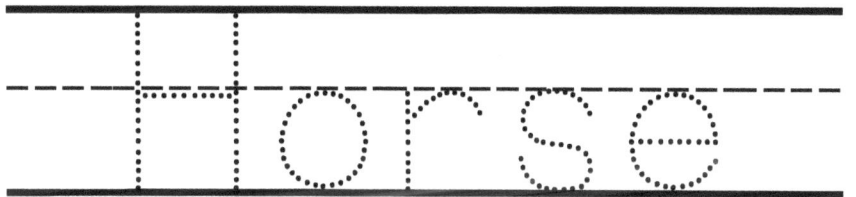

There are an estimated 99,000 horses in the state of Wyoming, and 6000 wild horses.

I

Islands

There are 32 named islands
in the state of Wyoming
on the many lakes.

J Jackalope

The Jackalope is a mythical creature thought to have originated in Douglas, Wyoming.

K

Kid

The Sundance Kid
took his nickname
from Sundance, Wyoming.

L

Lake

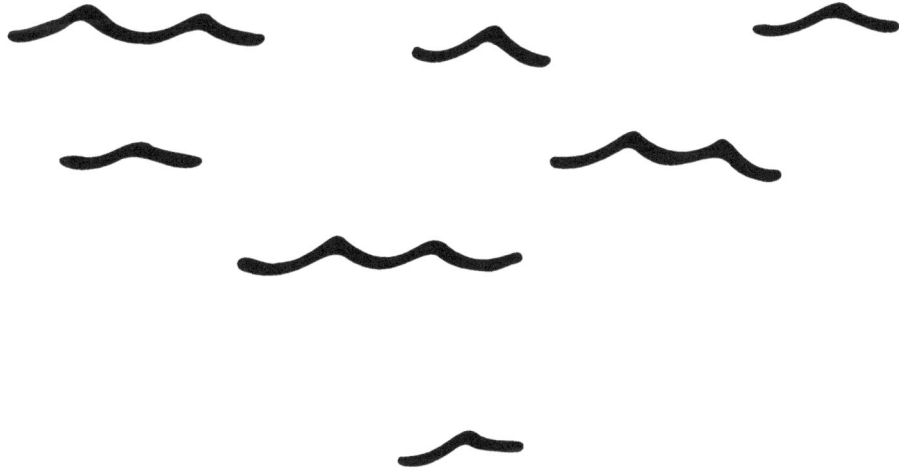

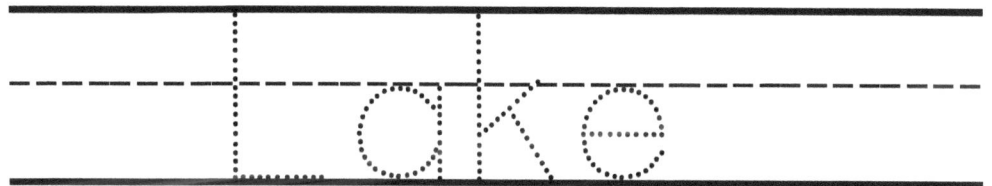

There are over 4,000 lakes and
reservoirs in Wyoming,
with lots of fishing!

M Mountain

There are 109 named mountain ranges in the state of Wyoming.

N

Nellie Tayloe Ross

The first woman elected governor in the USA was the 14th governor of Wyoming from 1925 to 1927.

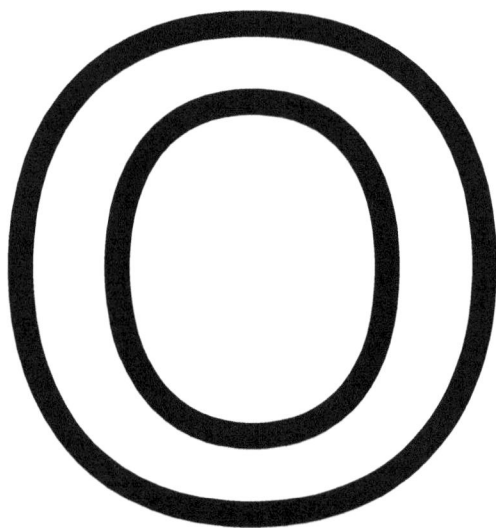

O

Old Faithful

Named in 1870 for the frequent and consistent eruption of the geyser.

P

Prairie

The prairies in Wyoming are below 7,000 feet in elevation and are mostly in the eastern part of the state.

Q

Quilt

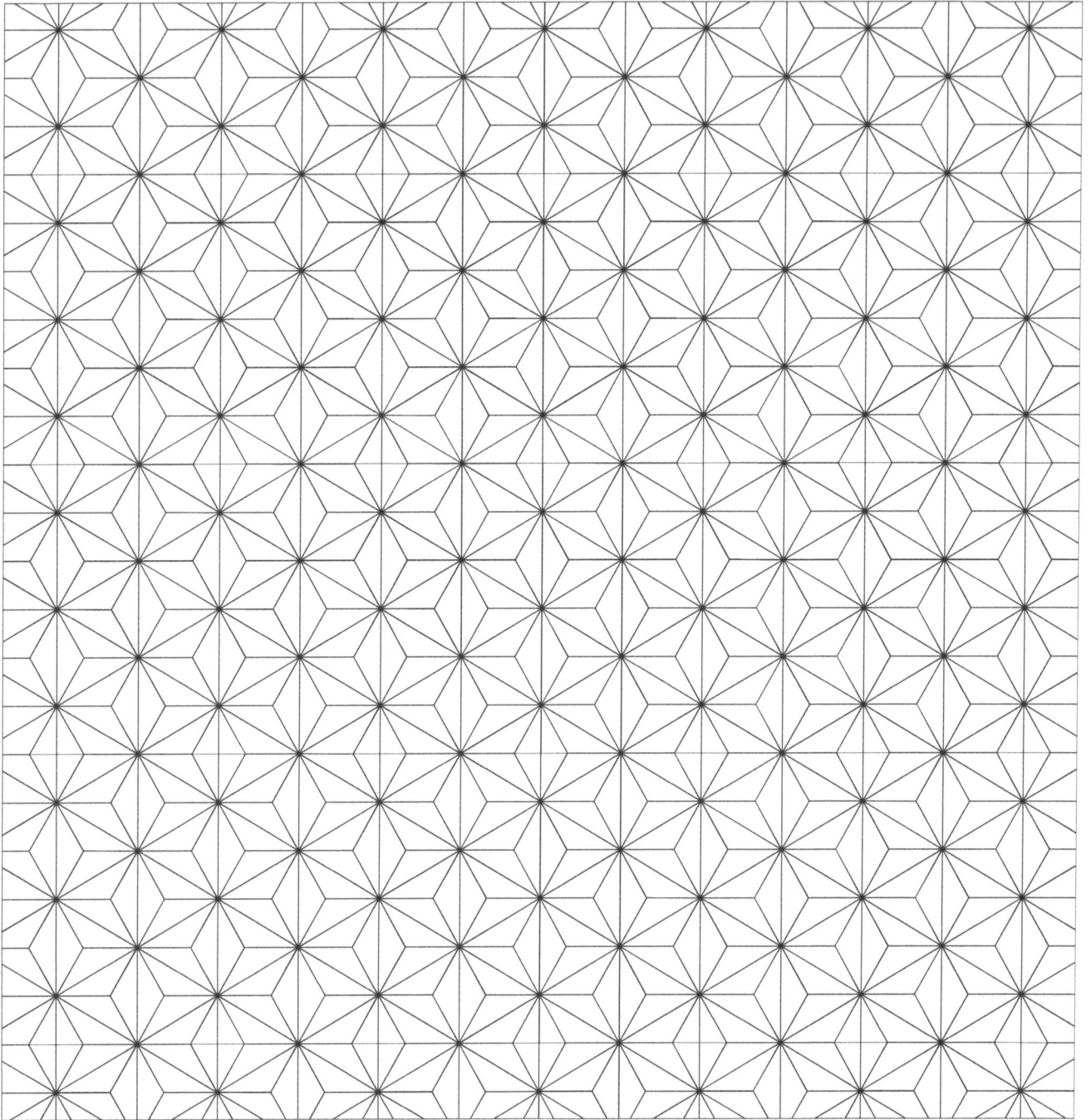

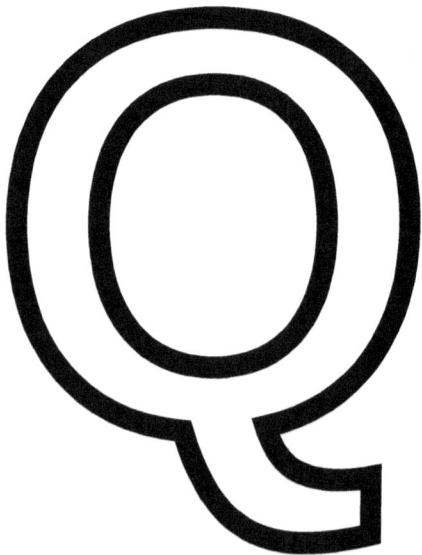

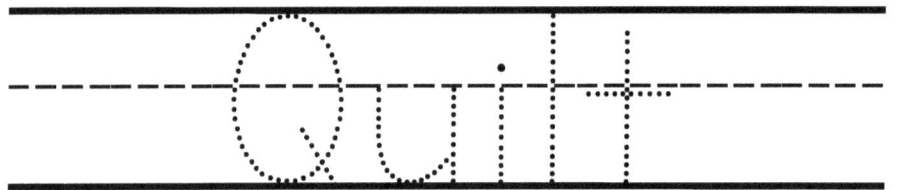

There are 28 quilt shops in Wyoming and a Quilt Trail near Lusk where around 100 barn quilts can be viewed.

R

Rodeo

Rodeo is the official state sport of Wyoming. Cheyenne Frontier Days is held every year (since 1897) in Cheyenne, Wyoming.

S

Snow

Moose, Wy gets the most snow at 170 inches of snow and Seaver, Wy gets the least at around 5.5 inches per year.

T

Tree

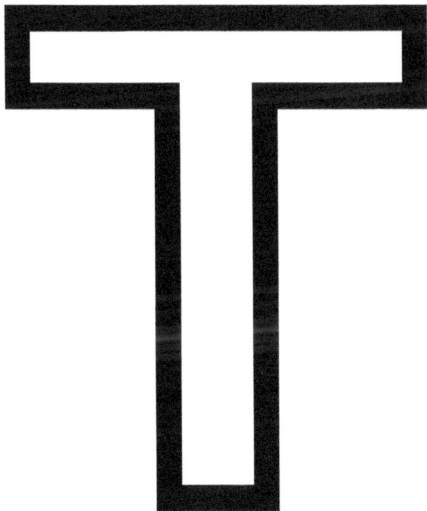

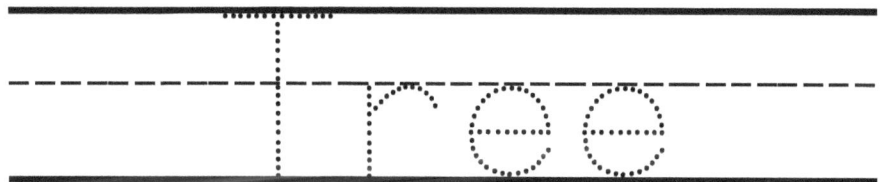

The Cottonwood tree is the
state tree of Wyoming, and is a member
of the willow family.

U

University

The University of Wyoming in Laramie
was founded in March 1886.

V

V̶a̶n̶ ̶T̶a̶s̶s̶e̶l̶l̶

With a population of 15, Van Tassell the least populous town in the least populous county in Wyoming.

W

Wolf

In the whole state, there are at least 314 wolves in at least 40 packs.

X

XX Ranch

It was the oldest ranch in Wyoming owned by the same family from 1868-1991.

Y

Yellowstone

The park was established in 1872 as the first National Park.

Z

Grizzly Bear

There are around 728 grizzly bears in Yellowstone National Park.

MY COUNT TO 10 WYOMING ANIMALS COLORING BOOK

name:

1

one bison

2

two meadowlarks

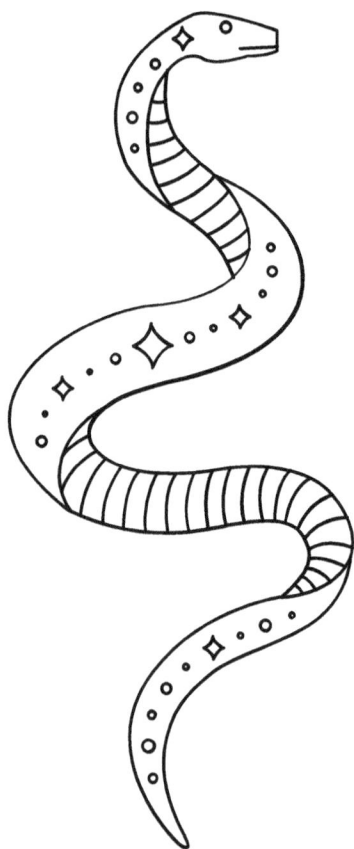

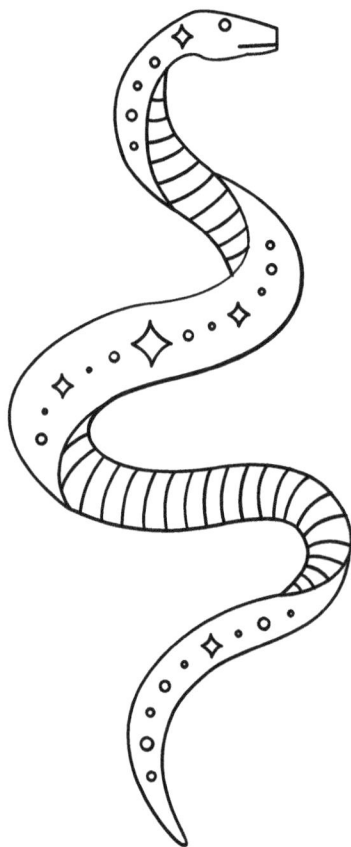

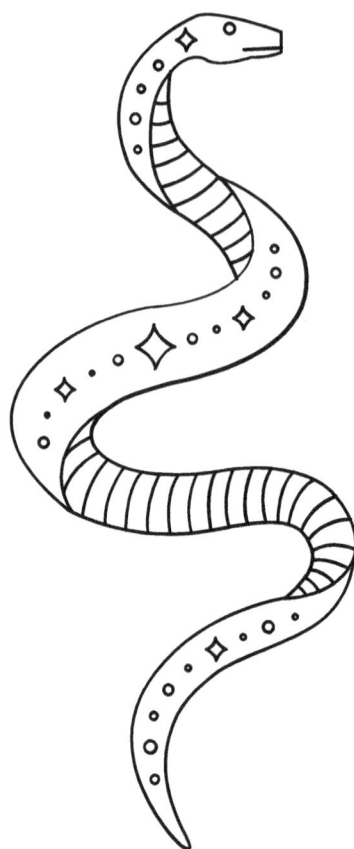

3

three snakes

4

four bears

5

five cows

6

six horses

7

seven elk

8

eight trees

9

nine deer

10

ten moose

Thank you for supporting our small family business!

Learn more at:

www.WyomingisHome.com

www.ingramcontent.com/pod-product-compliance
Lightning Source LLC
Chambersburg PA
CBHW042343030426
42335CB00030B/3444